SUPER SCIENCE
MICRO-ORGANISMS

Rob Colson

W
FRANKLIN WATTS

This edition published in 2013 by
Franklin Watts
338 Euston Road
London NW1 3BH

Franklin Watts Australia
Level 17/207 Kent Street
Sydney NSW 2000

Produced for Franklin Watts by
Tall Tree Ltd

Editor: Jon Richards
Designer: Jonathan Vipond
Photographer: Ed Simkins
Consultant: Ade Deane-Pratt

A CIP catalogue record for this book is available
from the British Library.

Dewey Classification 579

ISBN 978 1 4451 2293 9

Printed in China

Franklin Watts is a division of Hachette Children's
Books, an Hachette UK company.

www.hachette.co.uk

Picture credits:
Front cover: main image US National Institute of
Health, tr Martin Green/Dreamstime.com, tc Uwe
Kils, tr Jolynne Martinez/Dreamstime.com, 1 Mark
Lotterhand/Dreamstime.com, 3 Photomo/
Dreamstime.com, 4 Paul Harrison/GNU sharealike,
5t NASA, 5br Lyn Baxter/Dreamstime.com, 5bl
Monika Wisniewska/Dreamstime.com, 6b
National Institute of Health, 7t P. Rona, 7b Liv
Friis-larsen/Dreamstime.com, 8 US Gov, 9t E.R.
Degginger/Alamy, 9b Underumbrella/Dreamstime.
com, 10 KeresH/GNU, 11t Priscilla Spears, 11b
Christian Fischer/GNU, 12 USDA, 13t Nicu
Mircea/Dreamstime.com, 13b Mark Lotterhand/
Dreamstime.com, 14 NASA, 15t Darknightsky/
Dreamstime.com, 15b Jolynne Martinez/
Dreamstime.com, 17t Josef Bosak/Dreamstime.
com, 18 NOAA, 19t Uwe Kils/GNU Sharealike,
19b Uwe Kils/GNU Sharealike, 20 (from top)
Emanon/Dreamstime.com, Tom Dowd/
Dreamstime.com, Hans Hillewaert/ GNU
Sharealike, Øystein Paulsen/GNU, Damián H.
Zanette, 21t NOAA, 21b Alejandro Barreras/
Dreamstime.com, 22 Photomo/Dreamstime.com,
23t Jiri Flogel/Dreamstime.com, 23b Delft School
of Microbiology, 24 Dennis Kunkel Microscopy,
Inc./Visuals Unlimited/Corbis, 25t Eric Limon/
Dreamstime.com, 25b Josef Muellek/Dreamstime.
com, 26 Hixson/Dreamstime.com, 27t Ellington,
27b US Government, 28 Showface/Dreamstime.
com, 29t Peter Halasz/GNU Sharealike, 29b Elena
Elisseeva/Dreamstime.com

*Contents

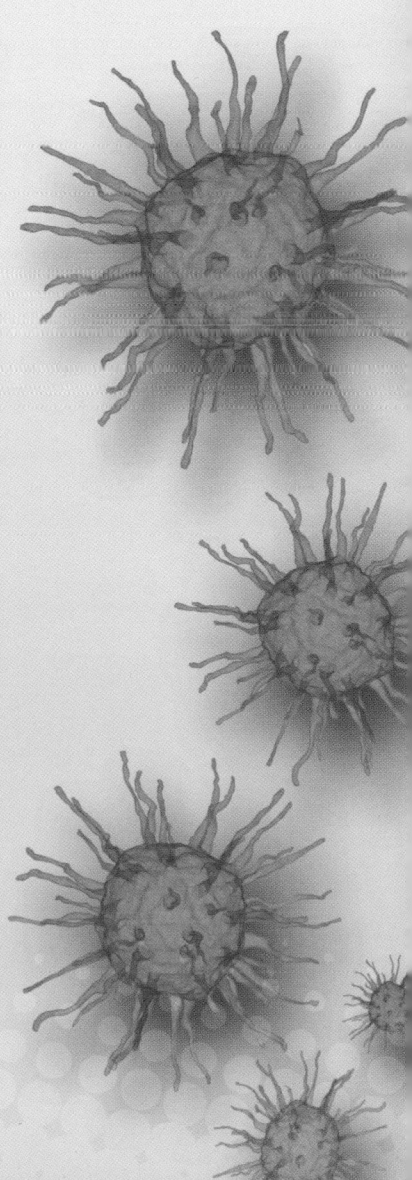

*What is a micro-organism?

Micro-organisms are tiny life-forms, most of which are too small for us to see. There are lots of different kinds of micro-organisms, including the smallest and simplest life-forms on Earth.

The first life on Earth

Life first appeared on Earth over 3 billion years ago in the form of microscopic bacteria. We know about early bacteria from the fossilised remains that have been found in ancient rocks called stromatolites. These tiny organisms were simple life-forms made of just one cell. A human body, by comparison, is made of over 10 trillion cells. The multi-cell life forms that would eventually evolve into us did not appear for another 2 billion years. Simple single-cell organisms are still the most common life-form on Earth, even though most of the time we are unaware that they are there.

Rocks called stromatolites formed from grains of sediment bound together by micro-organisms billions of years ago.

Is there life on Mars?

Photographs of the surface of Mars taken by the space probe Phoenix show a dry, rocky desert.

Generations of humans have gazed into the night sky and wondered whether there is life on distant planets. It is possible that there may be life on the planet nearest to us, Mars, in the form of tiny micro-organisms. For life similar to life on Earth to exist, liquid water needs to be present. Space probes have sent back images from the surface of Mars, and it appears to be very dry, but some scientists believe there may have been water – and life – on the surface of the planet in the past. Ice has been found, and there may be liquid water underneath the surface. Future missions plan to send probes that will drill deep below the surface to search for signs of life.

▌Studying micro-organisms

The study of micro-organisms is known as microbiology. Many micro-organisms are too small to be seen with the naked eye, so microbiologists use microscopes to study them. Before the invention of the microscope, nobody knew micro-organisms such as bacteria even existed. Bacteria were first observed in 1676 by the Dutch biologist Antonie van Leeuwenhoek, who used a simple microscope that he had made himself. Nowadays, scientists use powerful electron microscopes that can magnify an image by up to 2 million times.

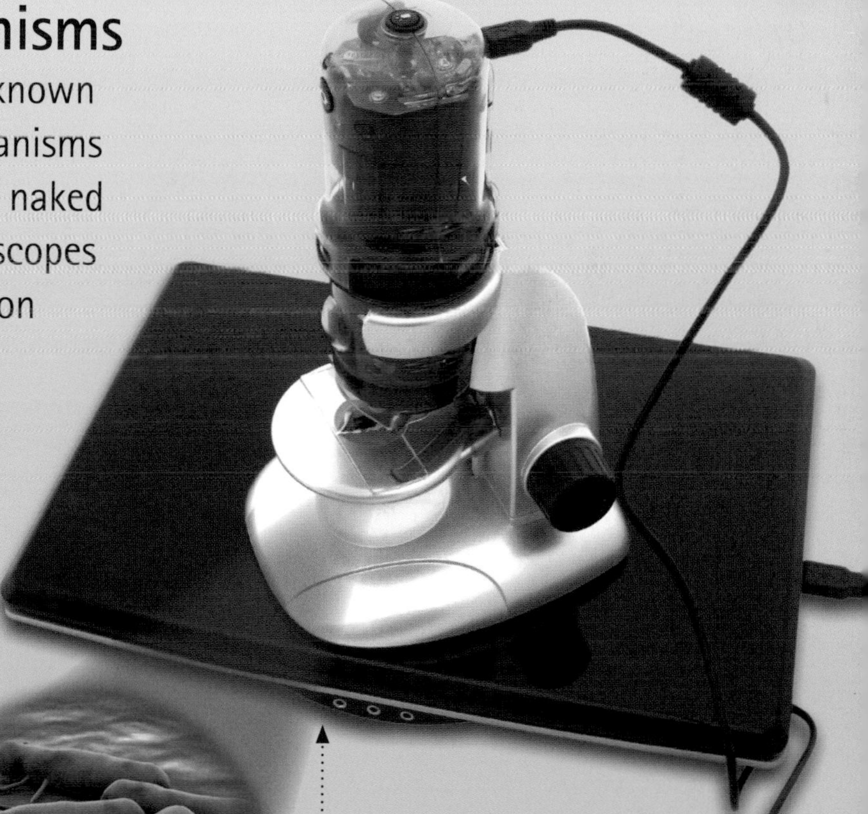

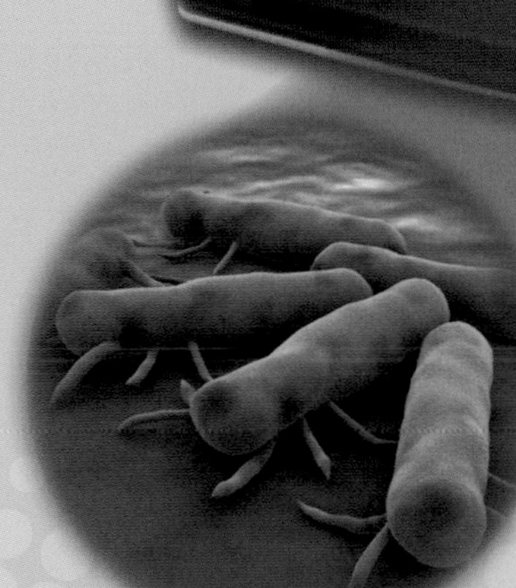

Electron microscopes produce an image by bouncing tiny particles called electrons off tiny objects such as bacteria.

*Bacteria and archaea

Bacteria and archaea are tiny single-cell organisms that we can't usually see, but are all around us. They are vital to all life on Earth, performing important functions such as recycling the nutrients in dead animals and plants.

The most abundant life on Earth

Bacteria are found on every continent from the hottest deserts to Antarctica, in every ocean, and even deep in the Earth's crust, up to 2 kilometres below the surface. Bacteria are tiny – about a million of them could fit on a pinhead – but all the bacteria in the world weigh more than all the animals and plants put together. In just one gramme of soil, there may be as many as 100 million individual bacteria. Some kinds of bacteria feed on other organisms, such as dead plants and animals. Others produce their own food using the energy of the Sun. Bacteria reproduce by growing and dividing into two.

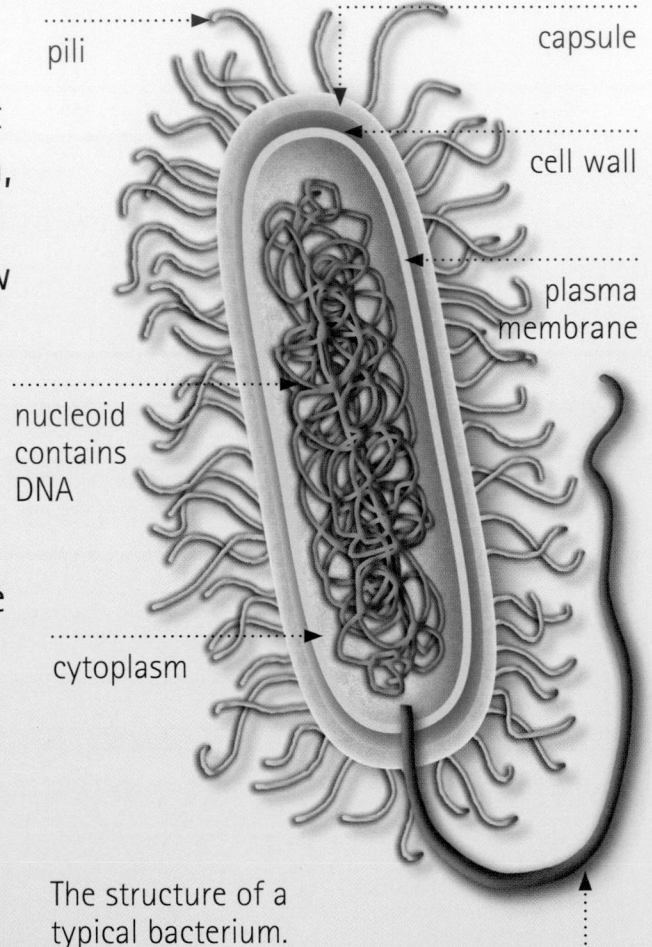

pili

capsule

cell wall

plasma membrane

nucleoid contains DNA

cytoplasm

The structure of a typical bacterium.

Tail-like flagellum moves bacterium along.

Bacteria come in many different shapes. Some are round, some are spiral, and others, such as these *Salmonella* bacteria, are rod-shaped.

Extremophiles

Archaea are organisms similar to bacteria that may have been on Earth for even longer. Many archaea are extremophiles, a name that means 'lover of extremes', which live in the harshest environments on Earth. Extremophiles have been found living inside rocks, in strong acids, very salty water and at temperatures of over 100°C. Some live deep in the ocean, where they take their energy from mineral deposits. If there is life on Mars, scientists think it is probably similar to archaea.

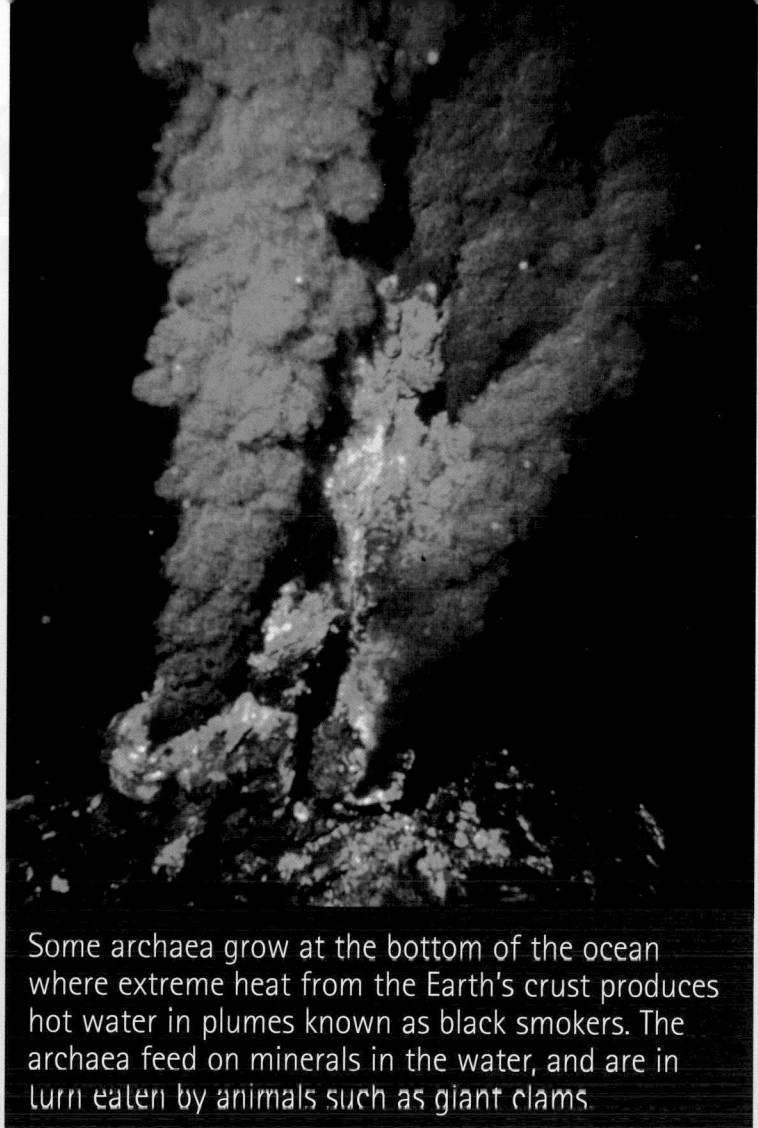

Some archaea grow at the bottom of the ocean where extreme heat from the Earth's crust produces hot water in plumes known as black smokers. The archaea feed on minerals in the water, and are in turn eaten by animals such as giant clams.

Project Make your own yoghurt

Milk is turned into yoghurt by bacteria. The bacteria eat the sugars in the milk and produce lactic acid, which thickens the milk and makes it into yoghurt. To make yoghurt, first clean a vacuum flask thoroughly. Ask an adult to rinse it with boiling water. This kills any bacteria that you don't want. Heat half a litre of full-fat milk until it is about 40°C, approximately body temperature. Add a tablespoon of live plain yoghurt ('live' means that it contains the living bacteria that you want), and pour the mixture into the flask. Leave the flask overnight for the bacteria to eat the sugars, and when you open it up, all the milk will have thickened into yoghurt.

Bacteria thicken milk into yoghurt by eating the sugars. Many people add sugar or fruit to yoghurt to sweeten it again.

*Protozoa

Protozoa are a diverse group of single-cell organisms that feed on smaller single-cell organisms such as bacteria. Without protozoa to eat them, bacteria would overrun the planet.

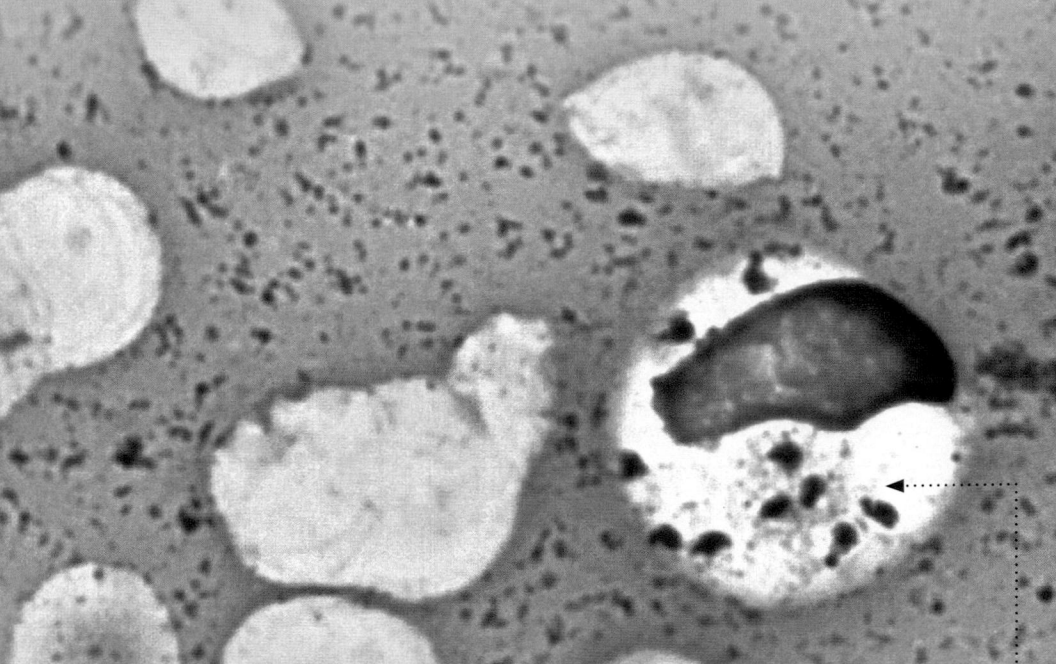

❙ Cells with a nucleus

Protozoa are more complex life-forms than bacteria. Inside all cells, a special chemical called DNA contains all the information for building and operating the cell. In bacteria, the DNA floats freely in the cell. In protozoa, the DNA is all contained in a central nucleus, which is surrounded by a protective membrane. When protozoa reproduce, they do so by making another copy of their DNA inside the nucleus before dividing into two new cells. This is the same way that the cells in plants and animals reproduce.

Some protozoa are parasites, which means that they live off other organisms. *Leishmania donovani* (the small blobs in the highlighted circle) is a kind of protozoa that spends some of its life inside human bone marrow cells.

Amoebae

Amoebae are the giants of the single-cell world. The largest amoebae may grow up to 5 millimetres long, although most are less than a millimetre. Amoebae live in the narrow films of water between soil particles. They move along these films in search of food, feeding on smaller protozoa and bacteria. Amoebae catch their prey using their remarkable ability to change shape. They extend two arm-like extensions, which join together to trap their victims under a dome, from which there is no escape.

Food is stored in vacuoles.

A membrane surrounds the amoeba.

An amoeba's 'arms' are called pseudopods, which means 'false feet'.

Studying protozoa

Protozoa live anywhere there is water, but are particularly abundant at the bottom of ponds. Collect a small sample of pond water by squeezing the water out of water plants such as pond weed, and take some of the plant with it. Put your sample in a shallow dish and carefully place a cover slip on the surface of the water. Leave overnight so that bacteria grow on the cover slip. The protozoa will come to feed on the bacteria. Carefully remove the cover slip using tweezers and lower it slowly onto a slide. Under the microscope, you should see a whole new world of tiny protozoa.

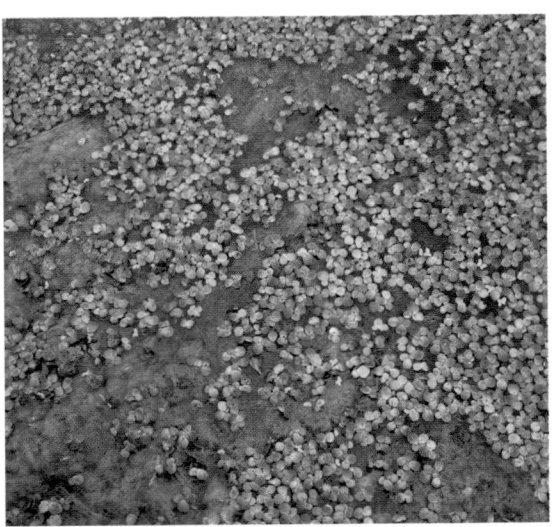

Large numbers of protozoa live on or near aquatic plants such as duckweed.

*Slime mould

Slime moulds are single-cell micro-organisms that spend part of their lives as tiny amoebae before coming together into a structure we can see.

The 'supercell'

Slime moulds are most often found on forest floors. In a kind of slime mould called a plasmoidal slime mould, thousands of individual cells are joined together to form one 'supercell', which moves across the ground feeding on other micro-organisms, and can grow to several metres across. Slime moulds begin their lives as single-cell amoebae. The single-cell organism fuses with another single cell if it finds a suitable one. The nucleus formed by combining the two cells divides repeatedly until there are thousands of nuclei within one large membrane – a slimy structure called a plasmodium.

Slime mould is aptly named. This one is called dog vomit slime mould, for obvious reasons.

Reproduction

A plasmodium will grow and grow, producing ever more nuclei as long as there is enough food for it to feed on. To reproduce, it moves to find open air and develops structures called fruiting bodies, which are often very brightly coloured. Once the fruiting bodies are fully developed, they lose their bright colour and release millions of spores into the air. If the spores land in a suitable moist place, they develop into the single cells that will form the next generation of slime mould.

This slime mould has climbed up the side of a plant pot, where it has formed its spore-bearing structure.

Project Grow your own slime mould

Growing your own gooey slime mould is very easy. You will need a *Physarum* culture (a small amount of a kind of slime mould, which you can buy as part of science kits), a Petri dish, filter paper and oatmeal flakes. Put the culture on the filter paper and place it in the Petri dish, then add a little water. Add a few oatmeal flakes. Cover the dish inside a resealable plastic bag to prevent it from drying out and put it in a dark container. Come back to the dish every day to check on its progress and add a couple more flakes when necessary as your slime mould grows. The flakes provide the slime mould with food, and it will continue to grow as long as you keep adding more flakes.

Physarum polycephalum growing in the wild.

Fungi

Fungi are a large group of organisms that include moulds (but not slime mould) and yeast. Many fungi live in the soil or on other organisms, and we often only notice them when they are producing spores in a spore-bearing structure such as a mushroom.

Spores

Fungi reproduce by producing spores, which they release into the air. Most of the spores will die, but a few fall in a suitable place to grow, such as on a piece of fruit. If you leave any food out for too long, mould spores will fall onto it and start to grow. Some kinds of cheese have mould introduced to them on purpose, and it appears in the cheese as coloured veins. These are special moulds that don't make you ill, but most moulds are not good for you, so avoid eating food that has gone mouldy accidentally and avoid breathing in the mould's spores, which can trigger asthma attacks.

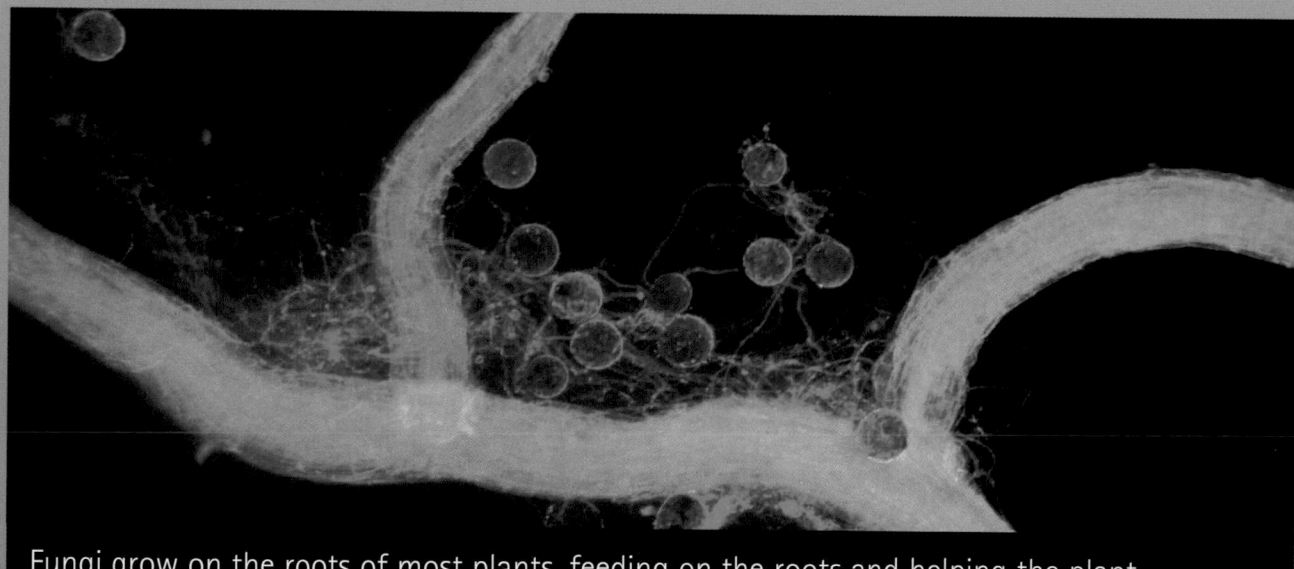
Fungi grow on the roots of most plants, feeding on the roots and helping the plant take nutrients such as nitrates from the soil, a mutually beneficial relationship called symbiosis. This image, taken under a microscope, shows fungus growing on a maize root. The spherical blobs are spores.

Fruiting bodies

Many fungi produce the tiny spores that will grow into new fungi in fruiting bodies. The fruiting bodies that we are most familiar with are mushrooms. Mushrooms are made by fungi that live underneath the soil. The spores grow on the underside of the mushroom cap, where they are carried off by the wind. Mushrooms grow in a couple of days and disappear just as quickly, but the fungus underground may live for many years. Never eat any mushroom you find in a field, as many are poisonous.

Mushrooms grow very quickly, and often appear overnight.

Yeast

A baker at work.

Yeast is a microscopic fungus that humans have used for thousands of years in baking and brewing. Yeast reacts with the sugars in food and produces alcohol and the gas carbon dioxide, a process called fermentation. Bakers add yeast to dough before baking it. Fermentation during baking produces bubbles of carbon dioxide in the bread, which make it light and spongy. Brewers add yeast to grain to make alcoholic beer. The soft drink root beer is made by a process of partial fermentation. Enough carbon dioxide is produced to make the drink fizzy, but only a small amount of the sugar in the root beer is turned into alcohol.

 Algae

Algae are micro-organisms that live in water and take energy from the Sun like plants. In fact, plants originally evolved from an ancient green alga. Algae vary a great deal in size and structure, ranging in size from tiny single-cell organisms to the large seaweeds.

A glowing sea

Algae use the energy of sunlight to grow, and some kinds of algae give off light themselves. At the surface of warm seas, single-cell algae sometimes live in vast numbers, called a bloom, with many thousands in every millilitre of water. Normally, these tiny cells are invisible, but when they are touched, they flash with a blue light. If you go for a swim in an algal bloom, your body will be surrounded by a warm blue glow. The algae do this as a form of warning, either to startle predators such as shrimp or to attract big fish to come and eat the shrimp that are eating them.

Glowing algae off the coast of Mexico tell fish in the area that there are shrimp here to be eaten.

Algae power

The world is running out of fuels called fossil fuels, such as petroleum and natural gas, and scientists are searching for alternative sources of energy to power our cars and machines. One possibility may be to make oil from algae to use as fuel. At the moment, crops such as soya beans are grown for fuel, but these crops take up valuable land and fresh water that could be used to grow food instead. Algae can be grown in salty seawater and even in dirty sewage water. In the future, vast algae farms in the sea may provide us with much of our fuel.

Algae thrive in the dirty water of sewage treatment plants. In future this algae may be used to make fuel.

Growing together

Lichens are small growths on the trunks of trees and rocks, which may look like flattened leaves, strands of hair or tiny bushes. In fact, they are a remarkable colony of fungus and algae. The two micro-organisms grow together in a partnership called symbiosis. The algae bring energy from the Sun to the partnership, while the fungus provides water and shelter. This powerful combination allows lichens to grow on solid surfaces almost anywhere in the world, including extremely cold places such as Antarctica. Colonies of lichen grow very slowly, as little as 1 millimetre a year, but can live for a very long time. Some lichens may be over 9,000 years old!

Lichen growing on the branch of a dead tree.

*Rotting and decay

When plants and animals die, their bodies are broken down into simpler forms of matter by micro-organisms. These simpler substances are recycled to provide the food and nutrients for the next generations of plants and animals.

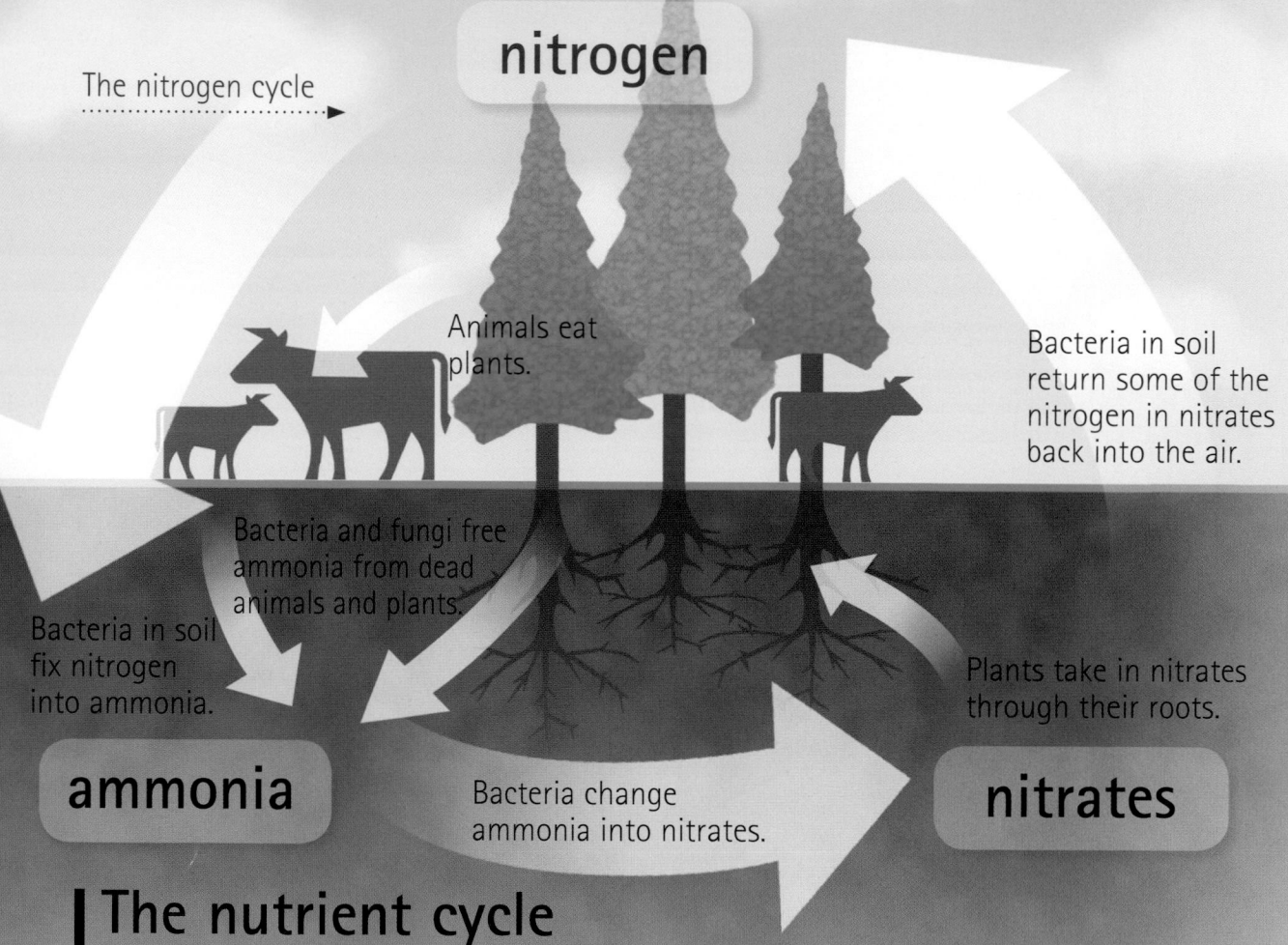

The nitrogen cycle

nitrogen

Animals eat plants.

Bacteria in soil return some of the nitrogen in nitrates back into the air.

Bacteria and fungi free ammonia from dead animals and plants.

Bacteria in soil fix nitrogen into ammonia.

Plants take in nitrates through their roots.

ammonia

Bacteria change ammonia into nitrates.

nitrates

The nutrient cycle

The movement of a chemical from living bodies to the earth or atmosphere then back to living bodies is called a nutrient cycle. One of the most important nutrient cycles is that of the chemical element nitrogen, which is found in all living things. About 80 per cent of air is nitrogen, but the gas has to be combined with oxygen to make nitrates before plants can use it. This process is carried out by bacteria, which also return nitrogen to the atmosphere. In this way, nitrogen passes through a cycle that makes life possible.

Decomposition

The process by which dead bodies rot and decay into simpler forms of matter is called decomposition. Bodies start to decompose as soon as they have died. Bacteria inside the bodies perform a vital role in the process, and soon start to release the gases that make dead bodies smell so rotten. Other micro-organisms in the air join in with the process, and fungi such as mould start to feed on the dead matter. Animals such as insects lay their eggs in dead bodies, and their feeding larvae speed up decomposition so that eventually all the nutrients in the body have been recycled and the body disappears completely.

This old lemon has started to decompose. The spores of mould in the air have landed on the lemon, and the mould is now feeding on it.

Project Decomposition in action

The bag on the left contains yeast, and the banana has gone brown and squashy as it decomposes more quickly.

Fungi such as yeast perform a vital role in decomposition. To see yeast in action, cut two slices about 2 centimetres long from a banana, and place them in separate clear plastic bags. Add half a teaspoon of yeast to one of the bags then seal them both up. Label each bag so that you know which one contains the yeast. Come back every day for the next four days and write down how each bag looks. Do the contents of the bags look different? Which piece of banana is decomposing more quickly? Throw the bags away at the end of the experiment.

Plankton

Micro-organisms that drift in the sea are collectively called plankton. Plant-like plankton are called phytoplankton, while the animal part of the plankton are called zooplankton.

Phytoplankton

Phytoplankton are a mix of micro-organisms, including bacteria, protozoa and algae, which all make energy from sunlight. They float near the surface of oceans and lakes, where there is plenty of light. Most phytoplankton are too small to be seen with the naked eye, but where they are concentrated in very high numbers, they may colour the sea green. The green colour is caused by a substance called chlorophyll, which is the same substance that makes plants green, and which they use to capture the Sun's energy.

Single-cell diatoms are one of the most common types of phytoplankton. They come in many different shapes.

Photosynthesis

Nearly all the energy we have here on Earth ultimately comes from the Sun. Plants and micro-organisms such as phytoplankton capture the energy in sunlight by a process called photosynthesis. About half of all the photosynthesis that takes place on Earth is done by phytoplankton. They use the energy they gain from photosynthesis to make proteins and other chemicals they need from minerals dissolved in the water. Ocean currents bring minerals such as nitrates and phosphates to the surface of the oceans from mineral-rich areas deep underwater.

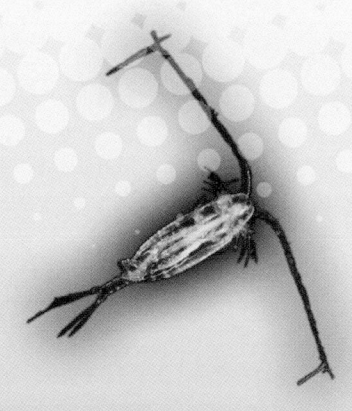

Copepods are a form of zooplankton found in every ocean and most rivers and lakes.

Zooplankton

Zooplankton are the animal life-forms that feed on the phytoplankton. They are a very diverse group of organisms, including jellyfish and tiny crustaceans such as copepods. The young, or larvae, of most fish start their lives in the zooplankton before growing into adult fish. Zooplankton cannot swim against the ocean currents, so they drift wherever the oceans take them. They come to the surface at night to feed on the phytoplankton, then sink into deeper water during the day to hide from predators.

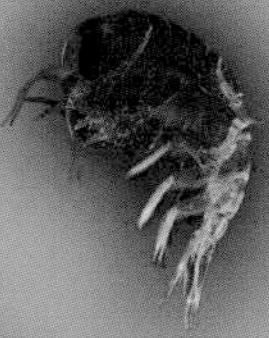

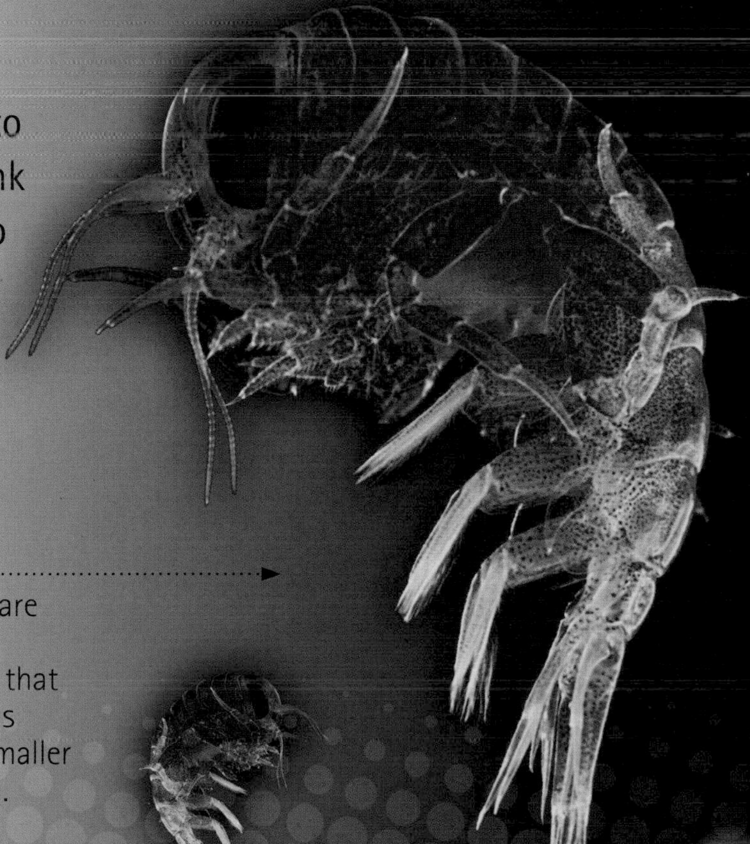

Amphipods are shrimp-like crustaceans that eat copepods and other smaller zooplankton.

*The food chain

All life needs food to survive. A food chain shows how each organism gets its food. Many organisms consume more than one kind of food, which means that each food chain forms part of a larger, more complicated food web.

▌Ocean food chains

All food chains in the oceans start with the phytoplankton, which are called producers because they make their own food. They are eaten by the zooplankton and small fish, which are called primary consumers. These are eaten in turn by larger fish and sea mammals, which are called secondary consumers. At each level of the food chain, energy is lost, which means that the higher up the chain you go, the fewer organisms there are at that level. So there are trillions of zooplankton in the sea, but only 100,000 killer whales.

An example of an ocean food chain.

killer whale

seal

small fish

krill (zooplankton)

diatom (phytoplankton)

Krill and blue whales

Some food chains are very short. Krill are small shrimp-like crustaceans, about 1 centimetre long, that form part of the zooplankton. Krill feed on phytoplankton, and are themselves eaten by the largest animal in the world, the blue whale. This enormous mammal grows over 30 metres long, but feeds exclusively on the tiny krill. The whales follow the krill into deep water during the day, and feed on them at the surface at night. Blue whales have a huge appetite, eating about 1,000 times more food than the average human. An adult whale may eat up to 40 million krill in just one day.

Tiny krill are the main food of the largest animal in the world, the blue whale.

The spring bloom

Every spring in the cold waters near the Poles, the phytoplankton bloom in huge numbers as nutrients from the bottom of the oceans are forced to the surface. This leads to a sudden rise in the number of zooplankton such as krill that feed on the phytoplankton. Many large animals, such as blue, humpback and right whales, have learned where and when the spring bloom will take place. The whales may travel thousands of kilometres to enjoy this annual feast.

Humpback whales feeding during the spring bloom.

*Viruses

Viruses are tiny organisms, most of which are about 100 times smaller than bacteria. They do not live independently, but reproduce inside other organisms.

Is a virus alive?

The structure of viruses is very simple. They contain genes made from either the chemical DNA or RNA, both of which are found in the genetic codes of cells. These genes are protected by a coat made of protein. Although viruses contain the genetic code for life, some scientists do not consider viruses to be alive. This is because they can only make copies of themselves inside the cells of other organisms. Other scientists believe that viruses are alive because they are able to reproduce and spread. Like other life, they are also able to evolve over time, changing to adapt to their surroundings.

Viruses can take many different shapes. This is a computer-generated illustration of the HIV virus, which causes the disease AIDS.

The life-cycle of a virus

Viruses need to get inside a cell to reproduce. When they encounter the right kind of cell, they attach themselves to its outside. From there they break into the inside of the cell, often leaving their protein coats outside the cell. Once inside, the virus's genes are released into the cell. The genes make copies of themselves with the help of the cell's machinery for making molecules. The new viruses this creates leave the cell by bursting its membrane, which kills the cell. Organisms can be killed by viruses that attack their cells in this way if they don't kill the viruses first.

A virus has attached itself to the side of a blood cell and is in the process of breaking through the cell membrane.

Martinus Beijerinck at work in his laboratory.

Germ theory

Infectious diseases such as influenza are diseases that can pass from one person to another. Before the 19th century, it was believed that many infectious diseases were caused by bad air. Now we know that they are caused by bacteria or viruses, an idea that is called germ theory. The German scientist Robert Koch proved that bacteria caused disease in the 1870s. Thirty years later, the Dutch scientist Martinus Beijerinck showed that tobacco mosaic disease, a disease that attacks tobacco plants, is caused by a virus.

*Micro-organisms in our bodies

Our bodies contain trillions of micro-organisms. In fact, there are more bacteria in our bodies than there are cells, many of them performing vital tasks that keep us alive and healthy.

An aid to digestion

There are many different kinds of bacteria in our stomachs. Like the bacteria that decompose dead bodies, the bacteria in our stomachs and intestines help break down our food into simpler substances, which we can then digest. Bacteria also help our bodies make vitamins, fight off disease and fight other harmful bacteria. Animals have different bacteria in their stomachs depending on the kinds of food they eat. Cows can digest tough grass in their stomachs with the help of their bacteria and other micro-organisms. We don't have the right micro-organisms to digest grass, but our stomachs are good at digesting beef!

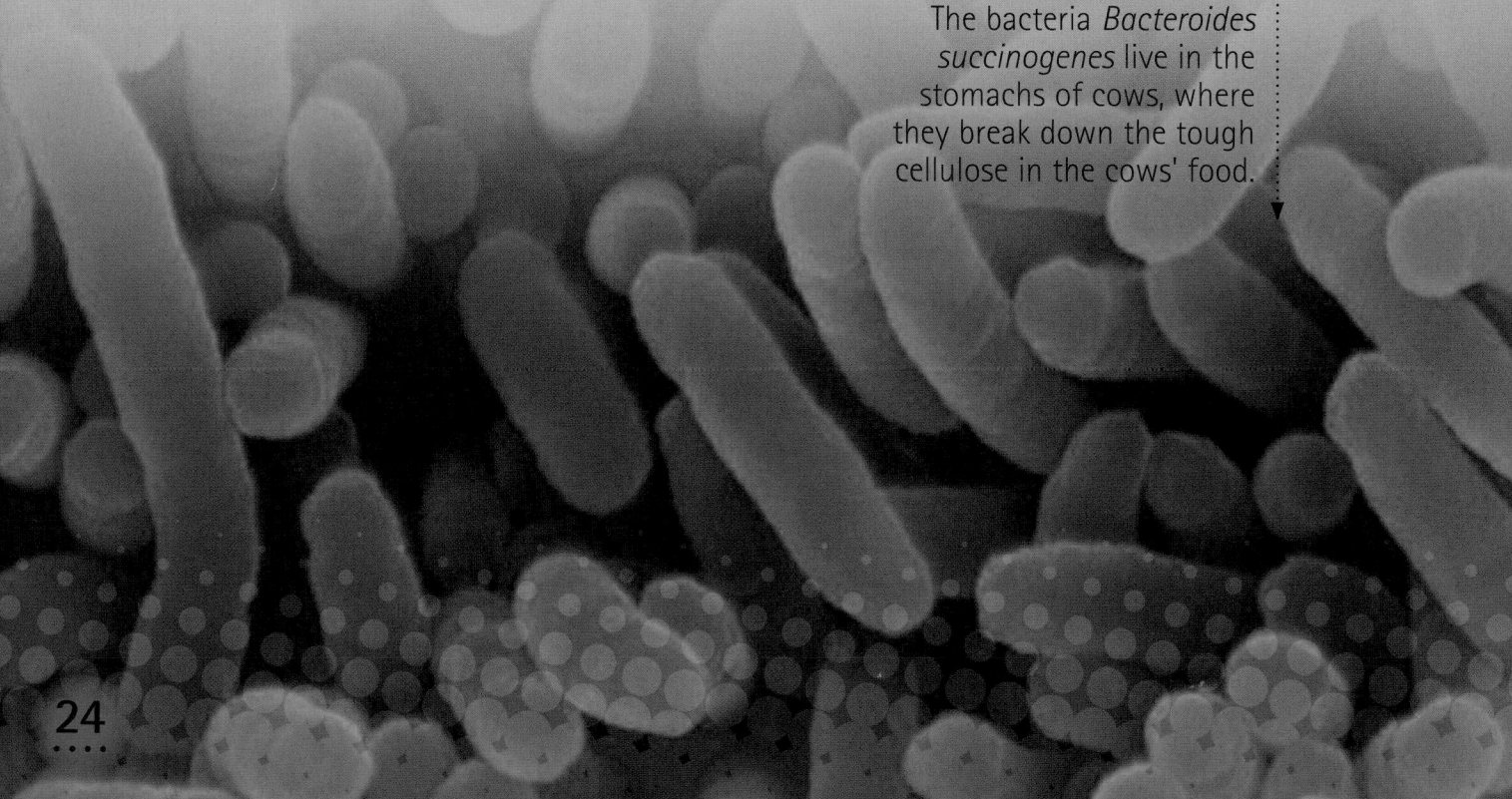

The bacteria *Bacteroides succinogenes* live in the stomachs of cows, where they break down the tough cellulose in the cows' food.

Bacteria on our eyes

Our eyes are protected from micro-organisms in the air by tear fluid. Tear fluid is very salty and few bacteria can live in it. It also contains chemicals called enzymes, which kill most of the bacteria that land on the eyes. One kind of bacteria, however, called *Corynebacterium xerosis*, can survive in tears. In return for a warm, moist environment in which to live, these harmless bacteria help the tears to fight off dangerous bacteria that cause diseases.

Corynebacterium xerosis live in the tear fluid that covers our eyes.

Project How clean are your teeth?

Bacteria love dirty teeth as there is lots of moisture and food for them to feed on. The bacteria quickly multiply to form a layer called plaque. Disclosing tablets stain plaque a bright colour such as blue. To see how clean your teeth are, put a disclosing tablet in your mouth for a couple of minutes, then spit it out, rinse your mouth with water and look at your teeth in the mirror. Wherever they are blue, there is plaque on your teeth. Brush your teeth thoroughly until all the blue has gone. Now you have clean teeth!

You should clean your teeth at least twice a day to remove the harmful bacteria that build up on them to form plaque.

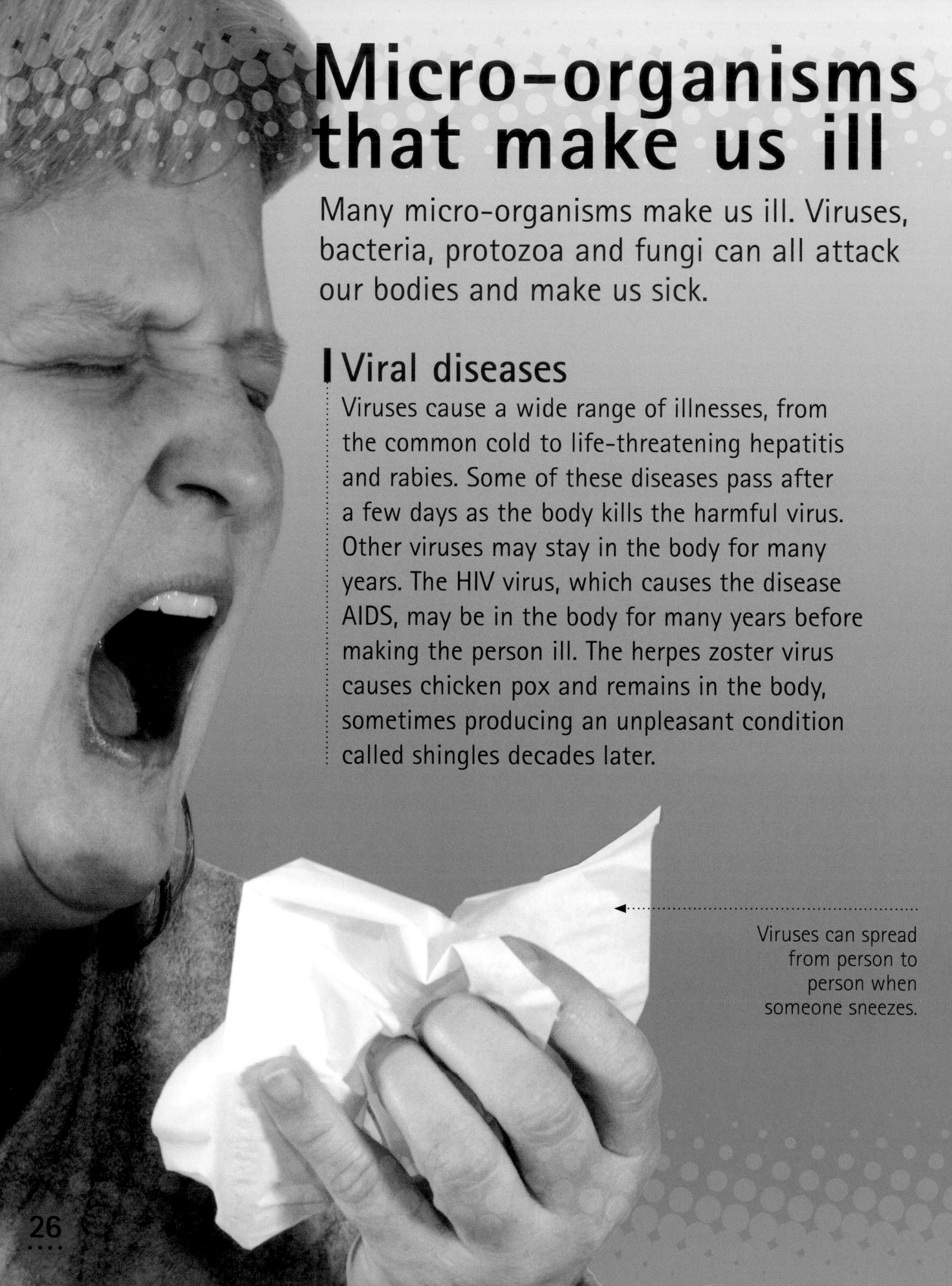

Micro-organisms that make us ill

Many micro-organisms make us ill. Viruses, bacteria, protozoa and fungi can all attack our bodies and make us sick.

Viral diseases

Viruses cause a wide range of illnesses, from the common cold to life-threatening hepatitis and rabies. Some of these diseases pass after a few days as the body kills the harmful virus. Other viruses may stay in the body for many years. The HIV virus, which causes the disease AIDS, may be in the body for many years before making the person ill. The herpes zoster virus causes chicken pox and remains in the body, sometimes producing an unpleasant condition called shingles decades later.

Viruses can spread from person to person when someone sneezes.

Fungal infections

Fungi most commonly infect the skin, where they feed on keratin, the protein that skin, nails and hair are made from. One common fungal infection called athlete's foot is caused by a fungus that lives in moist places such as our feet. Fungal skin infections are not life-threatening, but they can become very sore and itchy. Fungi like to grow in moist skin, so always make sure you dry yourself properly after taking exercise or having a bath.

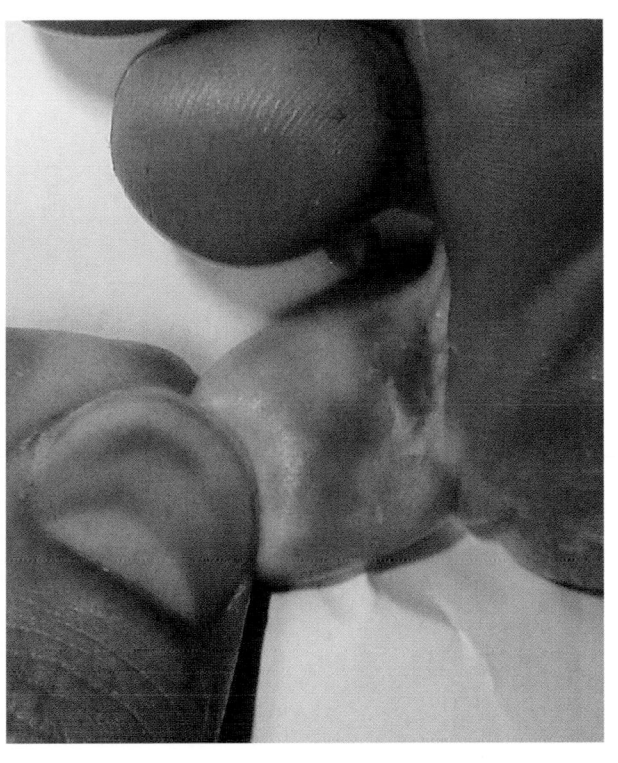

Athlete's foot is a fungal infection that grows in moist parts of the foot such as between the toes.

Bacteria and protozoa

Some of the deadliest diseases of all are caused by bacteria and protozoa. Bacterial diseases such as cholera are often caught by drinking dirty water. Dangerous bacteria are also found in faeces, which is why it is extremely important to wash your hands thoroughly every time you go to the toilet. Diseases caused by protozoa can be caught from insects. The disease malaria is caused by protozoa that live in some female mosquitoes. The mosquitoes bite us to drink our blood and pass the protozoa into our bodies as they drink.

Mosquitoes can pass on malaria when they bite us. Each year, nearly half a million people are infected with malaria by mosquitoes.

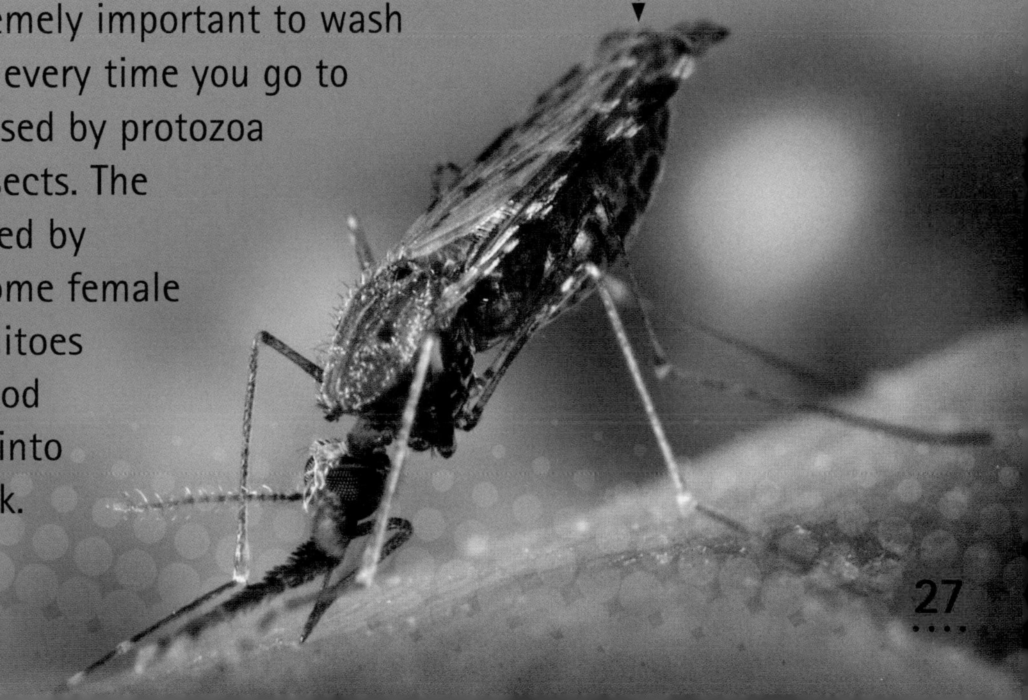

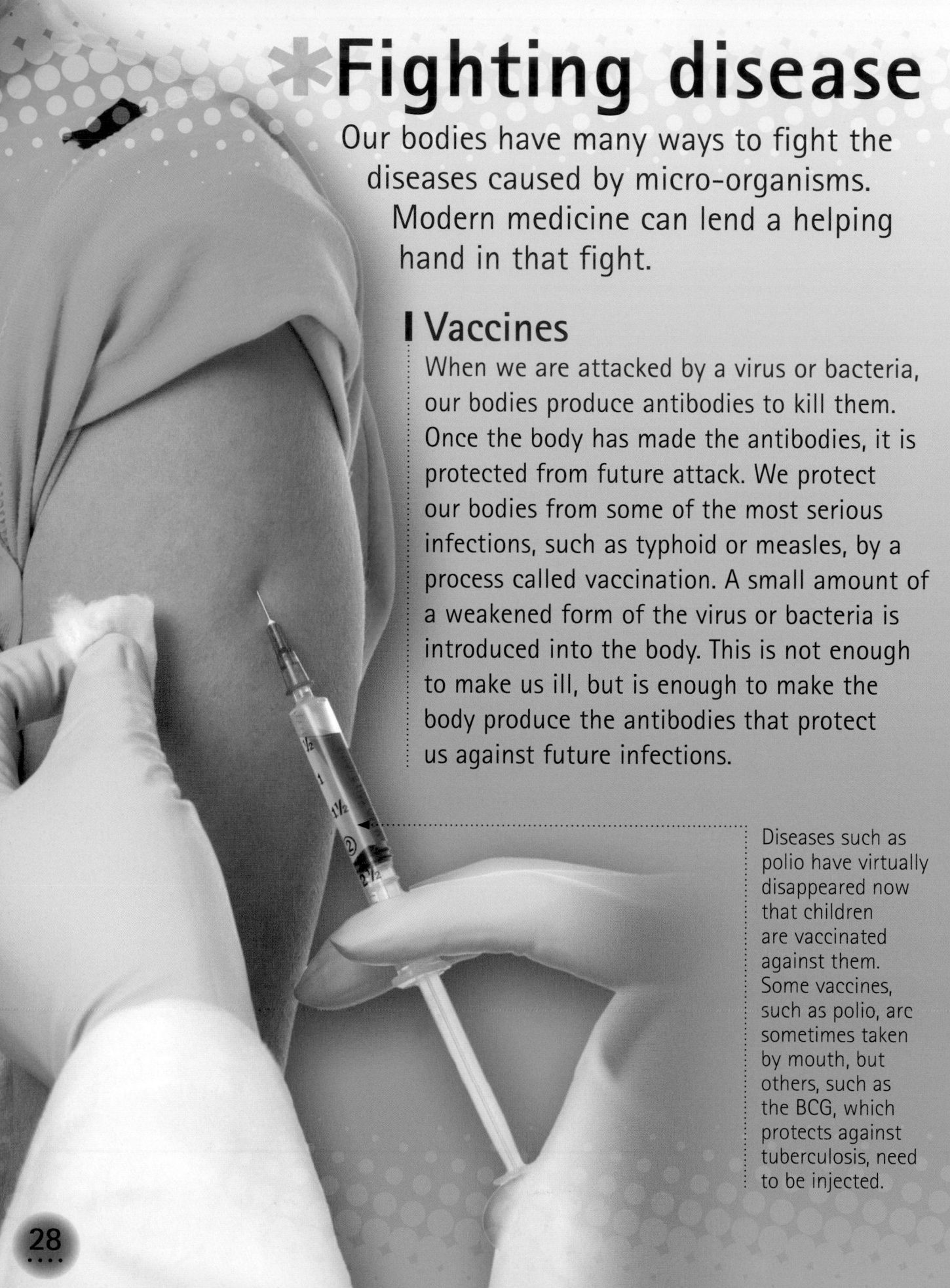

*Fighting disease

Our bodies have many ways to fight the diseases caused by micro-organisms. Modern medicine can lend a helping hand in that fight.

▌Vaccines

When we are attacked by a virus or bacteria, our bodies produce antibodies to kill them. Once the body has made the antibodies, it is protected from future attack. We protect our bodies from some of the most serious infections, such as typhoid or measles, by a process called vaccination. A small amount of a weakened form of the virus or bacteria is introduced into the body. This is not enough to make us ill, but is enough to make the body produce the antibodies that protect us against future infections.

Diseases such as polio have virtually disappeared now that children are vaccinated against them. Some vaccines, such as polio, arc sometimes taken by mouth, but others, such as the BCG, which protects against tuberculosis, need to be injected.

Antibiotics

Antibiotics are substances that kill bacteria. Our bodies naturally contain substances that kill bacteria, but we can be given antibiotics to help fight serious bacterial infections. One of the most important antibiotics, penicillin, is made from a fungus. Penicillin was discovered by accident in 1928 by Scottish scientist Alexander Fleming, who noticed that bacteria would not grow around a mould he was growing in the laboratory. Penicillin attacks many of the bacteria that make people ill and was the first good treatment for deadly diseases such as meningitis. It is now less effective as bacteria have evolved resistance to it, and new antibiotics have had to be developed.

A close-up of the fungus *Penicillum chrysogenum*, a type of penicillin.

Project Hot or cold water

The best way to kill bacteria on your hands is to wash them with soap and warm water.

Our hands can pick up lots of different kinds of bacteria, so we should wash them regularly. Hot water kills more bacteria than cold water. To see this, rub some glo-germ gel onto your hands. The gel will make any bacteria glow blue. Rinse your hands in cold water for one minute without rubbing them together. Now go into a dark room to see how much your hands glow. Next, rinse your hands for a minute in warm water and see how much they glow now. How much more effective was the warm water than the cold? Wash your hands with soap and water at the end of the experiment.

*Glossary

Cell
The smallest organised part of a living thing. The tiniest micro-organisms are made of just one cell.

Crustacean
An animal that has an external skeleton. Many species of zooplankton are crustaceans.

Decompose
To break down into simpler substances.

DNA
A long molecule inside a cell that contains the cell's genetic information, which tells it how to behave.

Infectious disease
A disease caused by micro-organisms, which can be passed from one person to another.

Life-cycle
The period from the start of an organism's life to the time it successfully reproduces.

Membrane
A protective layer. Cells are surrounded by membranes.

Microscopic
Too small to be seen by the naked eye.

Nucleus
The control centre of a cell, which contains the cell's DNA.

Organism
A living thing.

Protein
A chemical made from amino acids, which is essential to all life.

Recycle
To use again.

Sediment
Tiny grains of rock or minerals that are carried by flowing water, such as rivers, and are deposited on river and ocean beds when the water slows.

Spore
A single cell released into the air or water by many kinds of micro-organism in order to reproduce.

Symbiosis
A process by which different organisms live together and help each other.

*Resources

Up Close: Micro Bugs,
by Paul Harrison (Franklin Watts, 2007)
Fascinating facts about
micro-organisms, with superb
close-up photos on every page.

Germ Stories, by Arthur Kornberg
(University Science Books, 2008)
A Nobel Prize-winning scientist explains
the lives of micro-organisms in a series
of illustrated poems.

A World of Micro-organisms,
by Robert Snedden (Heinemann, 2007)
An exploration of the ways that bacteria
and viruses affect our lives.

Inside You, by Richard Walker
(DK, 2009)
An illustrated day in the life of
a human body.

The Horrible Science of Everything,
by Nick Arnold and Tony De Saulles
(Scholastic, 2008)
An exploration of the yucky side of
science, with a wealth of funny and
surprising facts.

Websites

www.childrensuniversity.manchester.ac.uk
Scientists from the University of Manchester
answer questions about micro-organisms,
with games to test your knowledge.

www.bigpicturescience.biz
A wealth of information and learning ideas
on micro-organisms.

www.ratlab.co.uk
Project ideas with an explanation of the
theory behind each one.

www.sciencewithme.com
Games and lots of science project ideas,
with worksheets and colouring books to
print out. A subscription website that's free
to join.

spikesworld.spike-jamie.com/science/
microorganisms
Ideas for projects that you can do at home.

www.scienceprojectideas.co.uk
Facts and trivia about micro-organisms.

*Index